T0113912

Without THE Smell OF Smoke

DIANNE CHATMAN

WESTBOW
PRESS®
A DIVISION OF THOMAS NELSON
& ZONDERVAN

WestBow Press books may be ordered through booksellers or by contacting:

WestBow Press
A Division of Thomas Nelson & Zondervan
1663 Liberty Drive
Bloomington, IN 47403
www.westbowpress.com
844-714-3454

All Scripture quotations are taken from the King James Version.

ISBN: 978-1-6642-5082-6 (sc)
ISBN: 978-1-6642-5084-0 (hc)
ISBN: 978-1-6642-5083-3 (e)

Library of Congress Control Number: 2021923742

Print information available on the last page.

WestBow Press rev. date: 11/30/2021

CONTENTS

DEDICATIONS

This book is dedicated to all those that be of the house of God and all those seeking to know the Lord Jesus Christ as their personal Savior, so that you will know that our God and faithful Savior stands with you in the fire and has the power and the ability to bring you out without the smell of smoke!

To God be, all the GLORY!

INTRODUCTION

*"The Righteous cry, and the LORD,
heareth, and delivereth them out of all
their troubles." – Psalm 34: 17*

The righteous cry, and the Lord hears them, is one
of the advantages or benefits of being righteous
and having the privilege of crying unto God, or
of calling on His name, with the assurance that
He will hear us and deliver us. They sing a song
in church by a preacher Joseph Scriven who
originally wrote it as a poem in 1855 to comfort
his mother in Ireland. The tune to the hymn was
composed by Charles Crozat Converse in 1868,
and William Bolcom composed a setting of the
hymn. It was published in 1865 by H. L. Hastings
with tune published 1870 by Oliver Ditson & Co.,
where one of the verses is, "What a privilege to
carry everything to God in prayer."

I have found that more often than not, we sometimes, as born again believers overlook the fact that it is a privilege to be able to carry everything to God in prayer in expectation that God will hear us and deliver us, because we are His children and He does love and care about our welfare. He is not just some idol man made god that does not exist and cannot save us, He is real and He alone has the power to deliver and save us from whatever the trouble, the attack, destruction, or plan of the wicked to hurt or destroy God's people. God and God alone, has the power to bring us out of any situation, trouble, or devastating event without the smell of smoke or being burned by it. Yes when we are in the midst of things it may look or seem that we are without help or the ability to deal with or handle the situation, but that's where prayer or our cries unto the Lord come in and our faith in God to deliver us, knowing that as He said in His word He would do, never leave us nor forsake us - Deuteronomy 31: 6, Hebrews 13: 5. This is the God we serve. He is not some make believe, cultic driven, manmade idol or man for that fact, that wishes to be worshipped like a god. Nor is He a fallen angel or principality, or darker power trying to exert some false rule, leadership or authority over man. He is GOD and GOD alone, and He is more than able to deliver us out of the fiery furnaces of life!

1

A STAND OF FAITH

"Nebuchadnezzar spake and said unto them, Is it true, O Shadrach, Meshach, and Abed-nego, do not ye serve my gods, nor worship the golden image which I have set up?

Now if ye be ready that at what time ye hear the sound of the cornet, flute, harp, sackbut, psaltery, and dulcimer, and all kinds of musick, ye fall down and worship the image which I have made; well: but if ye worship not, ye shall be cast the same hour into the midst of a burning fiery furnace; and who is that God that shall deliver you out of my hands?

Shadrach, Meshach, and Abed-nego, answered and said to the king, O Nebuchadnezzar, we are not careful to answer thee in this matter.

If it be so, our God whom we serve is able to deliver us from the burning fiery furnace, and He will deliver us out of thine hand, O King.

But if not, be it known unto thee, O King, that we will not serve thy gods, nor worship the golden image which thou hast set up.

Then was Nebuchadnezzar full of fury, and the form of his visage was changed against Shadrach, Meshach, Abed-nego: therefore he spake, and commanded that they should heat the furnace one seven times more than it was wont to be heated.

And he commanded the most mighty men that were in his army to bind Shadrach, Meshach, and Abed-nego, and to cast them into the burning fiery furnace.

Then these men were bound in their coats, their hosen, and their hats, and their other garments, and were cast into the midst of the burning fiery furnace.

He answered and said, Lo, I see four men loose, walking in the midst of the fire, and they have no hurt; and the form of the fourth is like the Son of God.

Then Nebuchadnezzar came near to the mouth of the burning fiery furnace, and spake, and said, Shadrach, Meshach, and Abed-nego, ye servants of the most high God, come forth, and come hither. Then Shadrach, Meshach, and Abed-nego, came forth of the midst of the fire.

And the princes, governors, and captains, and the king's counselors, being gathered together, saw these men, upon whose bodies the fire had no power, nor was an hair of their head singed, neither were their coats changed, nor the smell of fire had passed on them.

Then Nebuchadnezzar spake, and said, Blessed be the God of Shadrach, Meshach, and Abed-nego, who hath sent His angel, and delivered His servants that trusted in Him, and have changed the King's word, and yielded their bodies,

that they might not serve nor worship any
god, except their own God." – Daniel 3:
14 – 23, 25 – 28

This to me was a challenge of their faith in their God to deliver more than anything else, as well as how committed they were to their God. They not only stood on their faith, but they stood up for their faith. True it is hard to find such faith in many of the houses of God these days, but God is bringing an new awakening to the church were as, it is going to be established beyond a shadow of a doubt. If you want to be considered a child of the King, you are going to have to stand up and make your choice.

Now there are those making a stand every day for Jesus in countries that are against Christianity as well in countries that are for Christianity, there is still a remnant of believers that still love the Lord God with all their heart, mind and soul, and have not fallen prey to this world and its ways. There are still a remnant of true Christians that love God with all their heart, soul, and mind. There are true Christians around the world risking their lives every day from week to week to get the gospel of Jesus Christ, salvation out unto others. Standing before others and speaking the truth and what thus say the Lord in the face of adversity, putting their lives in their hands, to reach as many souls as possible and to all who will listen. The enemy doesn't limit his reach of benign influence to just those countries that are against Christianity, the adversary's influence over weak and idle minds is everywhere, but thank God, so is the power of God and through Christ Jesus!

These three young men having been taken capture by the Babylonian army were thrust into an environment that was both hostile towards their faith and their people. They had to learn how to make a stand without compromising their belief and faith in God. It reminds me of that passage of scripture found in – Ephesians 6: 10, 13, 14(a);

> *"Finally my brethren, be strong in the Lord, and in the power of His might.*
>
> *Wherefore take unto you the whole armour of God, that ye may be able to withstand in the evil day, and having done all, to stand.*
>
> *Stand therefore"- Ephesians 6: 10, 13, 14(a)*

They made a stand and because of it they were

thrown into the fire. We know that as Christians we have an enemy his name is Satan and he stands against everything that is God or pertains unto God! Every Christian around the world at some point or time in their lives will go through a trial by fire. Now it may not be a literal fire, but the effects are the same. Fire consumes causes pain, agony, and suffering! The fiery trials that come from the enemy are meant to destroy, but for the love of God as 2 Corinthians 4: 7 – 10, so aptly states;

> *"But we have this treasure in earthly vessels, that the excellency of the power may be of God, and not of us.*
>
> *We are troubled on every side, yet not distressed; we are perplexed, but not in despair;*
>
> *Persecuted, but not forsaken; cast down, but not destroyed;*
>
> *Always bearing about in the body the dying of the Lord Jesus, that the life also of Jesus might be made manifest in our body." – 2 Corinthians 4: 7 – 10*

We have a treasure, "the excellency of the power of God", that no matter what the enemy throws at us as long as we put our faith and trust in the Lord we will come out without the smell of smoke! These three Hebrew young men did not have the born again experience or the indwelling of the Holy Spirit through the receiving of the Holy Ghost Baptism to empower them spiritually as we have through the Lord Jesus Christ and still they took a stand on nothing but their faith, belief, and their commitment to God. These three young men exemplified the passage in 2 Corinthians 4: 7 – 9. Though they did not have the treasure in their earthen vessels the dying of the Lord Jesus at that time, yet they manifested the word in their faith, belief and their willingness to stand for that which was righteous and true, the one and only true God.

This attack was not only against the three Hebrew boys but also against the Jews as a whole, if God had not of stepped in to save the three young men from the flames, this would have been the fate of all the Jews who did not bow down to the image that Nebuchadnezzar had set up. This attack by the enemy, Satan, was meant for a nation's termination! After all, we as Christians know who is really the behind the influence and the attempt to stop the worship, belief and faith in God from going forth.

> *"Wherefore at that time certain Chaldeans came near, and accused the Jews." – Daniel 3: 8*

Had not Shadrach, Meshach, and Abed-nego not stood up and withstood the King, it would have led to dire consequences for all the Jews. Their freedoms would have been taken away from them forever if they bowed or their death if God did not intervene. This isn't just a story of the bravery of three young men, but of a saving of a nation! Every trial or challenge that Daniel and these young men faced was not only for them but for the nation of Israel. The enemy was after all the Jews and was trying to work through the few that were in leadership positions to justify their wickedness of coming out against all the Jewish people in captivity. Every time we face a trial it is never just about us. When we go through these trials by fire, we need not think this is just about us, it is always the bigger picture Satan is after. I believe these young men understood the demoniac attack they were under, that this was not just focused upon them, but on their belief in God as a people and they did not fail to stand, nor did they back down or bow down to the pressure or the threat upon their life, not even to the carrying out of the threat. They stood their ground because they understood, the bigger picture, if they bowed down then all Israel would have been forced to bow down or be destroyed just as well. If the Son of God did not intervene it could have been the death of a nation. The Jewish people would have been gone and we would not have the salvation of Jesus Christ today to save us from the judgment of eternal death today. That is what Satan was after when he rose up against the Jews through these certain Chaldeans by singling out the three young Hebrew young men, to stop the Messiah from coming through. Using the jealousy and the envy of the Chaldeans, Satan saw an opportunity to try and strike at the Jewish nation as a whole through and by attacking these three young men. Well, the plan failed because of the stand of true faith and commitment to God, these three young men made in refusing to bow down to an image made by man!

So many times we compromise our faith by bowing down to things that are not of God instead of taking a stand for righteousness. Like abortion for one which is looked upon as one sacrificing their children to the spirit of Baal, just like many of the Israelites where doing before they were judged by God and where taken into captivity by the Babylonians, the murder of unborn children. Same sex marriage which is considered abomination by God, man with man, woman with woman. All came from bowing down to that which was not God. When many in the church let their standards down and began to close their eyes to these things, or chose not to acknowledge the fact that these things were going on focusing on the number of members, money, buildings, schools, businesses, and the promoting of self instead of God, the Spirit of the Lord Jesus Christ, and have allowed that which was not holy or godly to go on in our churches, we opened the door for Satan to take a seat of authority in the house of God. Through our unwillingness to see, act upon or acknowledge the Holy Spirit and the will of God in the church, now these things have become an hindrance and a stumbling block to the saints of God in the body of Christ. Like these certain Chaldeans their jealousy and opened a door for the enemy to come in and seek to do evil against the Jews, but because of the intervention of the Son of God in the fiery furnace and because these three young men took a stand for God, they were given even more favor than they had before.

In this life we are going to have trials, tribulations, and challenges against our faith, but it is how you handle them, how you come out of them and how you go through them that matters to God. Do you lean on Jesus or do you lean on yourself and others, other than God. Are you going to stand on His word or are you going to try and stand on your own without God or just bow down to the influences and the pressures of the enemy and a fallen society and not take a stand for God at all, these are the choices.

2

STANDING IN THE FACE OF INTIMIDATION

"Then was Nebuchadnezzar full of fury, and the form of his visage was changed against Shadrach, Meshach, and Abed-nego: therefore he spake, and commanded that they should heat the furnace one seven times more than it was wont to be heated.

And he commanded the most mighty men that were in his army to bind Shadrach, Meshach, and Abed-nego, and to cast them into the burning fiery furnace.

Then these men were bound in their coats, their hosen, and their hats, and other garments, and were cast into the midst of the burning fiery furnace." – Daniel 3: 19 – 21

Isn't it funny how that when the enemy cannot convince you to bow to his will or cause you to become fearful, in order to get you to bow to his will, he immediately tries to intimidate you. Doing his best to strike out at you, attack you, or try to shame you or embarrass you into submitting to his will. Nebuchadnezzar knew that stripping these three young men down and binding them in their own clothing was an act of intimidation and to make them look ashamed before others, tit for tat, so to speak, no doubt Nebuchadnezzar felt much embarrassed and ashamed when these three Hebrew young men stood up to him in front of his court and still would not bow and were not afraid to tell him they were not bowing! In Shadrach, Meshach, and Abednego's stand for the right to bow and to worship God, they reminded the king of his place, nothing and no one is greater than God! No doubt this was a great slap in the face to someone that was being revered like he was a god before his people. Being unable still to make them bow, he became enraged. Now you have an enraged king, and much embarrassed king, and a very much set in his place king! Here sat king Nebuchadnezzar the conqueror of the known world at that time set in his place by three Hebrew boys!

> *"Now if ye be ready that at what time ye hear the sound of the cornet, flute, harp, sackbut, psaltery, dulcimer, and all kinds of music, ye fall down and worship the image which I have made; well: but if ye worship not, ye shall be cast the same hour into the midst of a burning fiery furnace; and who is that God that shall deliver you out of my hands?" – Daniel 3: 15*

Nebuchadnezzar truly thought at that time that his authority was greater than God's! Often time men and women forget that it is God who sets Kings up and it is God who brings them down! None of us are where we are in any given moment of life without God's knowing of it. As Christians we should always remember, God operates in two wills; His permissive will- which gives us the freedom to chose, and His Divine will- which deals with righteousness. God allows us the freedom of choice, but, He reminds of the consequences of wrong choices and decisions as well as the blessings of right choices and decisions in Deuteronomy 28. Just like there is light and dark, there is right and wrong. It is up to us to choose well.

Let us remember back in – Daniel 2:47, Nebuchadnezzar had just admitted to Daniel that his God is a God of gods, and a Lord of Kings! How quickly he forgot that Daniel was Hebrew just like these three young men and served the same God.

> *"Shadrach, Meshach, and Abed-nego, answered and said to the king, O Nebuchadnezzar, we are not careful to answer thee in this matter.*
>
> *If it be so, our God whom we serve is able to deliver us from the burning fiery furnace, and He will deliver us out of thine hand, O king." – Daniel 3: 16 - 17*

Wow! How bold is that?! But that is exactly the boldness that God requires of His people, unwavering boldness in faith in God. I remember having to have that boldness of faith one time in my life when facing an attacker concerning my faith in God, and yes it was a matter of my life. I remember I had not long had been saved and filled with the Holy Ghost when this challenge came to me. When facing one who was threatening my life because of my faith in Jesus, I told them that my God would protect me from them and if He chose not to, it didn't matter because I knew where I was going! I remember them looking at me, surprised I said what I said, they wasn't expecting that. They thought they could back me down under threat of my life. Well, I didn't back down and I am not going to back down now. Like the three Hebrew young men, it is not about the furnace, it is about God and whom will you serve, God or man? That day just like the three Hebrew young men, I saw the Lord intervene and do something supernatural right before my eyes which scared my attacker off and they ran from that which protected me, instead of me running from them! The Son of God went with the three Hebrew boys in the fire, and God's angel stood up and fought for me and protected me from my enemy that day! And I got to see it with my own eyes! It has emboldened me ever since! That was years ago, and I still believe in the delivering power of Christ and the protection of God the Father today! Truly He is more than the world against us! Even before I gave my life to Christ, God's destiny was over my life, I have faced guns before and after getting saved, and God's delivering power has been there with me through it all! I can understand the boldness of these three young men having watched the favor of God work in their life just like I have watched it work in mine, making a stand for righteousness and the right to worship the one and only true God, and not some manmade image, or idol or law! Once you have experienced the truth! It is hard to go back to serving a lie!

> *"For it is impossible for those who were once enlightened, and have tasted of the heavenly gift, and were made partakers of the Holy Ghost,*
>
> *And have tasted the good word of God and the powers of the world to come,*
>
> *If they should fall away, to renew them again unto repentance; seeing they crucify to themselves the Son of God afresh, and put Him to open shame." – Hebrews 6: 4 – 6*

These three young men had tasted that God was good and worth standing for and if necessary, the giving of their lives for, and decided amongst themselves that they would not bow! I say again what a display of strong stand of faith in God!

"But be it known unto thee, O King, that we will not serve thy gods, nor worship the golden image which thou hast set up." – Daniel 3: 18

No fear! No hesitation, no doubt in God's ability to save them if He so pleased! Just true unadulterated faith in God! How wonderful is that?! These young men knew of the command to bow down and worship the image of gold that the king had set up and they also knew of the punishment which would come from not bowing down. I am sure they were aware of the jealousy of these certain Chaldeans that were around them, watching them, and no doubt understanding that it might, would mean their lives for disobeying the king's command, had already decided amongst them that they were going to make a stand and follow God no matter what knowing the God that they served! They might have even prayed to the Lord about it before hand, when they decided to make their stand. It reminds me of a gospel song wrote by Crystal Lewis – I Must Tell Jesus;

I must tell Jesus all of my troubles,
I cannot bear these burdens alone,
In my distress He kindly will help me,
Jesus can help you, Jesus alone!

Well guess what? Jesus, the Son of God, did help them, Jesus alone. No doubt that at some time they knew that they might be coming for them because of their not bowing down and worshipping the image of gold when the music played. They had already made their choice. This is something that we as Christians should decide to do every day, make a decision to stand and not to bow to the will of the enemy!

Well, neither Nebuchadnezzar's threat nor his intimidations of stripping them of their garments and tying them up in their own garments worked! When you know the God you serve, no matter what manner of tactic or intimidation is going to make you look feel ashamed before others, why? Because there is nothing to be ashamed of when you are standing for God! Whether you are stripped bare or left with everything! There is no offense in serving God.

One wonders why the furnace was commanded to be heated seven times more than needed.

According to Babylonian mythology there were seven demons known as "Maskim" who were worshipped by the Babylonians for supposedly having infernal powers. Maybe this was done in reference to the these seven demons that the Babylonians worshipped and because of the religious offense of the unwillingness of the three Hebrew young men to bow down and worship the image that Nebuchadnezzar had set up, and the ridiculous command of heating the furnace seven times. The enemy is never pleased when one takes a stand for God and always looks for ways in which to try and intimidate the one who has made a stand. Nebuchadnezzar at first tried to offer them an opportunity to bow, thinking that they may have just not understood what they were being commanded to do and possibly because of the position in which he had placed them in, no doubt feeling like the three young men owed him some allegiance or obedience to bow down and worship the image he had set up. When this did not happen he became enraged being brought to open embarrassment before his own court.

Nebuchadnezzar did not understand that any promotion that these young man were given was not because of him, but because of the favor of the

Lord, and the Lord proved it, by intervening in the fiery furnace and the promotion these three young men received after they were brought out. Notice the clothing that was stripped off of the young men was the clothing that was provided for them by the king when he first placed them into their offices of authority in the Babylonian kingdom. This is what was stripped off and used to bind the young men up in, meaning that this is what would be burned first! It is almost like saying how the plans of the enemy are the first things to go! What was left was of God.

The urgent request was made for the furnace to be heated not because there was no rope to be found to bind the young men to put them in the furnace or change their clothing. The hat was taken off, that representing the enemies authority over them, the coats were taken off, representing the enemies covering over them, the hosen or under garments were taken off, stripping off the last bit of influence the enemy could have had over them and then they were bound with them to show the offense that was felt because of the refusal to bow. It makes one ask the question, were there not plenty of rope to bind the young men with? I am sure in the time it took to find the mightiest men in the Babylonian army to get there to throw the young men in the furnace, somebody could have found some rope! But because this was a religious offense as well as a offending of one's pride and position, Nebuchadnezzar wanted to make a show of things as well as try and prove some mute point that His false gods were greater than the one true God! Didn't work! How do I know this you say? By the comment that was made later on in the story, which is why I deem this as a challenge of faith. All throughout the Word of God we see men and women of God faith being challenged not by God but by the enemy, God knows His people.

Just like in the book of Job, God knew why Satan had came up with the sons of, because he had tried to come against Job and God had put an hedge around him because Job faithfully served God and honored Him. God allowed Satan to test Job because He knew Job. He knew that Job would not stop serving Him. So the challenge of will Job was, would he continue to serve God in the midst of trials and loss. The devil threw everything at Job. Job loss all he owned, his cattle, his herds, his camels, his servants and his children. The last thing that Satan touched was his health and Job still did not lose his integrity in God nor blame

God foolishly for what was happening to him, even when he did not understand why or wherefore, he still did not blame God foolishly. Job stood on his integrity, what he knew about God. Satan tried to break Job, make him turn against God. He thought that if he took away everything that Job had he could break him. When that did not work, he went back before God to petition to touch Job's health. He gave him the most painful and humiliating sickness disease as he could. Job's body outwardly where covered with boils in which worms crawled in and out of his body. His body also carried an putrid odor because of the draining of fluids, which was coming from the boils that covered his body. All that Job had once owned and was precious to him was taken from him, even his sons and daughters. Those within the city whom he had helped forsook him. No one wanted to be around him. Even his own wife told him to curse God and die because she could no longer stand to see him suffering. Job was left sitting in sackcloth and ashes. His so called, three friends who claimed they came to comfort him, instead began to steady falsely accuse him. Arguing that he must have done something wrong before God as to the reason why he was suffering. Trying to make him admit unto it, instead of comforting him they compounded his misery! That was just as bad as the king telling Shadrach, Meshach, and Abednego, I am going to give you one more chance to bow down to this false image or die! That's like telling someone, I'm going to give you one more chance to choose to go to Hell and burn in the lake of fire! Where you will burn throughout all eternity, forever feeling the pain and torment of an unquenchable flame! As opposed to burning for a hot minute for your stand for God! Then going up to heaven where you will never have to suffer pain or disappointment ever again, living in the eternal bliss of God's presence, joy, peace. Never having to ever again experience any sorrow, grief or despair what so ever again, much less an attack from the enemy! Which one would you choose?

"And fear not them which kill the body, but are not able to kill the soul: but rather fear Him which able to destroy both soul and body in hell." – Matthew 10: 28

These three young men made a choice. They chose to obey God. They faithfully obeyed the first commandment of God, **"Thou shalt have no other gods before me" – Exodus 20: 2 – 5;**

"I am the LORD thy God which brought thee out of the land of Egypt, out of the house of bondage.

Thou shalt have no other gods before me.

Thou shalt not make unto thee any graven image, or any likeness of any thing that is in heaven above, or that is in the earth beneath, or that is in the water under the earth.

Thou shalt not bow down thyself to them, nor serve them: for I the LORD thy God am a jealous God, visiting the iniquity of the fathers upon the children unto the third and fourth generation of them that hate me;" - Exodus 20: 2 – 5

They did not let the threat of death, nor, the intimidation and fury of the king cause them to turn away from serving the one and true God, and Him alone. They stood and were faithful and obedient to God and because they stood, God stood with them.

The enemy comes to steal, kill, and destroy our faith, trust in God, our belief, worship, praise, and our service to God. If he can in any way deceive you, seduce you, intimidate you, or persuade you to bow down to anything but God, he knows he has you, unless you stand, and stand therefore!

How many today are willing to stand in the face of adversity As I look back over my life and see all the times I had to stand in the face of adversity and challenges to my faith and what I had to go through and even endure until the Lord delivered me, I know that beyond a shadow of an doubt, that it was Jesus who stood with me in the midst of the furnace. I have even had times when I was told that even if I mentioned the name of Jesus it could have been my death. I can still remember when it happened. I was starring down the barrel of a loaded 45, pointed at my head. I started to calling on Jesus in my mind and I remember seeing a fiery lined shield, like clear glass come down from above, open and unfold like a page of a book right in front of me. I heard a voice say, "This is the Lord, tell them if they fire the gun, that it was going to backfire upon them and blow up in their face, and if they did not believe it, to fire the gun." There I was defenseless of any weapon, except for an open Bible on Psalm 91 which I held pressed against at my chest! Standing on and in faith and the power of my God to help me, I repeated what the voice of the Lord told me to say to the perpetrator, not knowing how they were going to receive it. To my surprise but overwhelming gratefulness to the Lord, they dropped their arm, still holding the gun, their eyes got big as they looked up as if looking over my head! With a face full of fear, they called me crazy, and ran off! I don't know what they had seen after I told them what the Lord told me to tell them, maybe, one of God's holy angels protecting me, but whatever, or whoever they saw, it frightened them to no end! God is good!

I did not stop calling on Jesus just because a gun was being pointed at my head, nor was I going to back down off of my salvation for any witch or warlock! There is only one king and one God in my book! God the Father, one king, Jesus the Christ! There is no other name, person, place or thing that we as Christians should be bowing down too, but the name of Jesus!

3

GOD'S ANSWER TO THE KING'S CHALLENGE

"Therefore because the king's commandment was urgent, and the furnace exceeding hot, the flame of fire slew those men that took up Shadrach, Meshach, and Abed-nego.

And these three men, Shadrach, Meshach, Abed-nego, fell down bound into the midst of the burning fiery furnace.

Then Nebuchadnezzar the king was astonied, and rose up in haste, and spake, and said unto his counsellors, Did not we cast three men bound into the midst of the fire? They answered and said unto the king, True, O king.

He answered and said, Lo, I see four men loose, walking in the midst of the fire, and they have no hurt; and the form of the fourth is like the Son of God." – Daniel 3: 22 – 25

This was not only about the saving of the three young Jewish men from the flames of the furnace, and a people from the destruction, but of the validity of the power of God, the one and only true God to be able to save His people! God answered Nebuchadnezzar's challenge of, "Who is that God that shall deliver you out of my hands?" in a most supernatural way! He not only appeared in the fire with the three young men, but He also would not let the fire burn the men nor the smell of the smoke linger on their bodies or their garments! Their hair was not singed! Nor their bodies burned, plus He freed them to walk around in the flames giving all the more praise unto Him! This reminds me of the verses in – Isaiah 43: 1 - 2, where the Lord was speaking to Israel through the prophet Isaiah:

"But now thus saith the LORD that created thee, O Jacob, and He that formed thee, O Israel, Fear not; for I have redeemed thee, I have called thee by thy name; thou art mine.

When thou passest through the waters, I will be with thee; and through the rivers, they shall not overflow thee: when thou walkest through the fire, thou shalt not be burned; neither shall the flame kindle upon thee." – Isaiah 43: 1 - 2

Being this prophetic word was given to the people of Israel before they went into captivity in Babylon, these three Hebrew young men may have been taught the writings of Isaiah at some time in their life, or by unwavering faith in God, decided to make a stand for God trusting in Him for their deliverance and if God chose not to deliver, remain faithful until the end. Not everyone has to face challenges like these, but for those who end up in situations where they do, we have to make the right choices or decisions for our soul's sake, knowing that whatever way the Lord leads, it will always be to our blessing, whether we live or whether we die! Paul sought to leave this earthly realm and be with Jesus, was somewhat grieved because the Lord was not through with him yet on earth as of yet.

> *"For me to live is Christ, and to die is gain.*
>
> *But if I live in the flesh, this is the fruit of my labor: yet what I shall choose I wot not.*
>
> *For I am in a strait betwixt two, having a desire to depart, and to be with Christ; which is far better:*
>
> *Nevertheless to abide in the flesh is more needful for you." – Philippians 1: 21 – 24*

Who knew that this promise of God was actually going to be tested? Satan knew, because he was going to bring the test and God was ready for him! Do you not know that Satan has to bring everything he wants to do to the saints before God, before he is allowed to do it? The book of Job proved that, (Job 1: 6 – 12). Also our very own words do the same. When we tell God that we would let nothing stop us from serving Him no loss, no one! The devil hears us and goes before

God to get permission to try you at your words! Thank God for Jesus!

The enemy tried the three Hebrew boys at their word that they would not bow no matter what! Then the king put the challenge out to God to defy his,(the king), words and his assumed power over the mighty power of the God of Israel who as we know was and is the God over all! Talk about lifted up in ones' self!

You know once these three young men saw the Son of God appear with them in the fire, while experiencing and witnessing to the miracle that was being done unto them, you know beyond a shadow of an doubt it had to spark the praises of God from them! This had to be an amazing sight to behold for the king and all who were watching and witnessing this great wonder and obvious supernatural event taking place before their eyes! There was no doubt that the God of the Jewish people the God of the three Hebrew men was God, the one and only true God! This reminds me of the Elijah challenge on top of mount Carmel, when Elijah challenged the false prophets of Baal to have their god to burn up the offering, (1 Kings 18: 25 – 41). Which we know did not happen! Because God is God and there is no one beside

Him! Only the offering offered buy Elijah was answered with fire!

These three young men trusted in God! They knew that God was able to deliver them and if He did not, they were not going to disobey God and bow down to that which was not God! And God did deliver and caused the flames to burn those who had cast them in! God's justice will prevail. The Lord answered the challenge.

When Satan came before God concerning Job, God accepted the challenge and allowed Satan to test Job. As I stated earlier, Satan wanted to break Job, cause him to curse God. Now we know that this did not take place no matter how much suffering Satan put upon Job, Job held onto his integrity and did not curse God, even when in the midst of intense suffering when his own wife told him to do just that, wanting to see Job's suffering end. Even then when he had lost all, body diseased, sitting in sackcloth and ashes, in all this Job, sinned not!

> *"Then Job arose, and rent his mantle, and shaved his head, and fell down upon the ground, and worshipped.*
>
> *And said, Naked came I out of my mother's womb, and naked shall I return*

thither: the LORD gave, and the LORD hath taken away: blessed be the name of the LORD.

In all this Job sinned not, nor charged God foolishly." – Job 1: 20 – 22

Today, I am finding those who say they trust and love God, finding it hard to hold onto God and their faith in the lightest of trials and tests and are charging God for everything! You would think with all the churches that are in the world much less in the cities, all the Christian schools and seminaries, all the schools of theology, all the mega churches there would be a better report coming from the houses of God, but unfortunately, there isn't. Why is that, I wonder? Is it because the teaching and leadership, and counsel that many should be getting from Spirit of the Lord and in the anointing of the Holy Ghost is not going forth, because man in his press to be the center of attention, instead of giving it to God has left the Spirit, the true gospel of Jesus Christ as well as the truth and the Holy Ghost out of the church, could be. How about this, too much compromising with the world to "get along", not stir up any dust or trouble? But this is what the early church in the book of Acts was all about! Stirring up dust! And causing trouble for the kingdom of Satan! Jesus said in – Matthew 16: 18;

"And I say also unto thee, That thou art Peter, and upon this rock I will build my church: and the gates of hell shall not prevail against it." – Matthew 16: 18

Notice Christ said, "The gates of hell shall not prevail against it!" Not that you are fending off an attack from Satan, but that you are attacking Satan and his kingdom and its works! And that God had given you the power through the Holy Ghost to prevail! Who went down into hell to bring Christ back up after He died on the cross and was buried in the tomb and went down into hell to take the keys of death and the grave from Satan? That same power dwells in the saints of God today through our Lord and Saviour Jesus Christ and the power of the Holy Ghost.

When Jesus was brought before Pilate by the chief priests and elders of the people who had had taken counsel against Him, Pilate began to ask Him concerning the false charges that the Pharisees had brought against Him. When Jesus would not answer back, he told Him how that he had the power to crucify Him or release Him. – John 19: 11;

> *"Then saith Pilate unto Him, Speakest thou not to me? Knowest Thou not that I have the power to crucify Thee, and have power to release Thee?" – John 19: 10*

Now hear Jesus' answer:

> *"Jesus answered, Thou couldest have no power at all against me, except it were given thee from above: therefore he that delivered me unto thee hath the greater sin." – John 19:11*

"Thou couldest have no power at all against me except it were given thee from above". Jesus let Pilate to know that he really did not have any power over Him at all, unless God had given it to him or allowed it to be so. When the enemy brings a challenge against God or assumes a power that has not been given him by God, they force Him to answer! Pilate assumed a power he did not have, Nebuchadnezzar assumed a power that he did not have and challenged God! They both forced God to answer! Jesus quickly let Pilate to know that he had not the power to speak over the outcome of his life.

The three Hebrew young men let Nebuchadnezzar to know he did not have power over them as to the outcome of their lives, when they told him that God was able to deliver them and if not, or in other words, if God chose not, they still would not serve his idol gods. They recognized who really has the power over life and death, to say what the outcome will be, and that is God! This truth was personified in Christ in the statement He made to Pontius Pilate during His questioning. Think about it, Satan has no power over you but what God will allow. This was also proved with Job, though Satan not only wanted to vex Job, he also wanted to kill him. God told him what he could touch concerning Job and what he could not. God's final answer to Satan was, touch not his life. In other words, you are not allowed to take his life. Satan was not even given authority or power to touch anything about Job, he had to ask, and he presented it in a challenge:

"Doth Job fear God for nought?
Hast not Thou made an hedge about
him, and about his house, and about all

that he hath on every side? Thou hast blessed the work of his hands, and his substance is increased in the land.

But put forth thine hand now, and touch all that he hath, and he will curse thee to thy face.

And the LORD said unto Satan, Behold, all that he hath is in thy power; only upon himself put not forth thine hand. Satan went forth from the presence of the LORD." - Job 1: 9 - 12

You would have thought he would have known better, having been in heaven and around God, God never loses a challenge! Job came out more blessed than he was before! Everything he had lost was given back double. God gave him seven more sons, and three more daughters, that loved God, and there were no more beautiful in all the land than the daughters God gave back to Job for the sons and daughters that Satan had taken from him in his challenge to God. So God blessed Job's later end greater than his beginnings. Why? Because in all of Job's suffering, Job never charged God foolishly and he held unto his integrity, in other words, Job like the three young men kept to his faith and belief and trust in God and stood on what he knew about God!

The book of Job was written by Moses, so obviously somewhere in Moses' journeying he met Job and learned of his story. Having being told how the hand of God settled the matter and the challenge put forth by Satan unto God concerning Job, he no doubt being moved by the Spirit of God, wrote about it for people of all times could see how the hand of God moves in even our most devastating of situations where the God in us is challenged as to who He is, His power, and His authority over and in the lives of all mankind, as well as heaven and earth.

4

THE PROOF IS IN THE DELIVERANCE

"Then Nebuchadnezzar came near to the mouth of the burning fiery furnace, and spake, and said, Shadrach, Meshach, and Abed-nego, ye servants of the most high God, come forth, and come hither. Then Shadrach, Meshach, and Abed-nego, came forth of the midst of the fire.

And the princes, governors, and captain, and the King's counselors, being gathered together, saw these men, upon whose bodies the fire had no power, nor was an hair of their head singed, neither were their coats changed, nor the smell of fire had passed on them.

Then Nebuchadnezzar spake, and said, Blessed be the God of Shadrach, Meshach and Abed-nego, who hath sent His Angel, and delivered His servants that trusted in Him, and have changed the King's word, and yielded their bodies, that they might not serve nor worship any god, except their own God." – Daniel 3: 26 – 28

I can just imagine King Nebuchadnezzar's facial expression when he looked into the furnace and saw Shadrach, Meshach, and Abed-nego walking around in the fire unharmed! Instead of witnessing some form of Babylonian dominance and watching the three young men burning for defying his command to bow down to the idol he had set up, he saw three young men walking around in the fire unharmed and praising the almighty God on high and guess what, the Son of God standing in the midst with them in the fire! Now you might wonder, why would they be walking around instead of still being bound in one place? God not only kept them from being burned, but He also freed them from the shame of being bound in their own garments!

What greater picture of being freed from one's sins is this? The garments that they wore were given them by the king of Babylon an idol worshipping nation, a fate brought on through being made captive because of the sins of their own nation Israel. Not only did the Lord not let them be burned by the flames, He walked with them in the fire, having freed them from bondage of the corruptness of Babylon in loosening their garments which had been used to bind them. God so established His point who should mankind really be worshipping and serving and that He was the one and only true God and divine power who is able to deliver or condemn, till the astonished King wanting to see this supernatural deliverance of the God of Shadrach, Meshach, and Abednego called for the young men to come out of the furnace.

Nebuchadnezzar might have also been expecting the fourth man, the Son of God who he saw walking with the three men to come out with them. The Lord having saved the young men openly, needed not to prove His point any further. The proof was in the deliverance! These three young men had stood the test, they did not bow, God had answered the challenge! The King had no other course but to believe what had been proven before his very eyes and not only his eyes but the eyes of all his princes, governors, captains and counselors, who had all gathered around to witness the burning, but instead witnessed a miraculous and supernatural event of God! What a humbling surprise that must have been for the King and his court! All got to witness the event. No doubt these burnings were made a public spectacle to establish the Babylonian dominance over their people or captives and all who do not bow to their gods or idols. This time it was God's establishment of Himself, the one and only true God! Where were the Chaldeans that had accused the young men then? Where was the fiery wrath of the King? What happened to the pride of the Babylonians? All died in the flames of the furnace! When God brought those three young men out of the flames of the furnace un harmed and without the smell of smoke, all doubts and all questions were put to rest in the flames of the furnace!

Isn't it something that when the enemy thinks he has the upper hand, and wants to show he has some kind of power over people, he believes in drawing a crowd to garner some unwarranted attention to themselves, they tend to make a big spectacle of things, like looting and rioting because they know it will make the news and others will blow it out of proportion, and yes, some will fear. Challenging the opposite party or parties to do something about it. This is in order to bring about a greater effect of the spectacle and establish some untruth. What the young men did was quell this type of thing happening from the beginning. These three young men by calmly, but firmly taking a stand against bowing down to the image that the king had set up and standing on the promise of God to deliver them and to be with them in the fire. Remember this was a persecution aimed at the Jews as a whole. These three young men were just singled out as an excuse or false reason to get it started, but God intervened. This wasn't just a rescuing of three young Jewish men, but a rescuing of the Jewish nation as a whole! This was another satanic attempt to stop God's plans to bring salvation into the world through Jesus Christ! If the Jewish nation had been killed off during Nebuchadnezzar's reign there would have been no releasing of the people after seventy years to rebuild the temple or the city of Jerusalem, because there would have been no people to go back! There would have been no Davidic lineage to bring the Messiah down through. The scepter would have ended there! But, as it says in the book of Isaiah 55: 11, God's word will not go out and come back void. Remember in Genesis 48: 10, the Lord guided Jacob (Israel), to bless his son Judah and his lineage with this blessing;

> *"The scepter shall not depart from Judah, nor a lawgiver from between his feet, until Shiloh come; and unto Him shall the gathering of the people be." – Genesis 48: 10*

This would have not happened if the command of Nebuchadnezzar for everyone to bow down to the golden image or be thrown in the fiery furnace had been allowed to stand whereas the Jewish people were concerned, because the enemy of God and God's people would have made certain that all the Jews were terminated because of this. These three Hebrew young men in standing stood for all of Israel. Through their willingness to stand on their belief and faith in God and obedience to God whether it meant their life or death, moved the Lord God to act on all of Israel's behalf and show up and deliver them in such a supernatural way, granting them the freedom of religion to serve their God and not have to bow down to any of Babylon idols or images. God in doing what He did in the fiery furnace proved His authority to the Babylonians over whatever demons and demoniac powers they were worshipping proving who is the all power for all time. So we see this is not just a battle fought on just the physical realm, but on the spiritual realm as well as the political. Satan heard the blessing spoken over Judah and has tried everything in his power to stop it. Failing, he even thought that the crucifixion would stop it. That didn't stop it either, because as we know, on the third day, Jesus rose from the grave with all power in His hands! God's will, will be done.

Most people do not look at this side of the matter. They just mostly center it on the young men, but I believe in reading the whole word of God. I have found if you do not take in the whole word of God you will miss a very important point. All of God's word carries mysteries to unfold! If the word of God had of just focused it on the three young men you would of known this was just a personal attack, but the seldom looked over scripture in the text whereas it states that the Chaldeans came near, and accused the Jews, not just the Chaldeans came near to accuse Shadrach,

Meshach, and Abednego, but the Jews. They were going to use Shadrach, Meshach, and Abednego, to get things started against the Jews as a whole. Satan trying to stop God's plans! Yes teaching of the three Hebrew boys stand is a great faith point, but the teaching on the deliverance is even a greater scan of things. There was more to this than three young men's deliverance! All of our deliverance and deliverances were involved in these three young men's stand of faith! For as you know it is because of the Jewish people we have Christ, and His salvation for all mankind or whosever was willing to receive it and it was through the lineage of Judah the promise of Jesus Christ the last and eternal King whose kingdom would have no end came into the world. This promise of God about the scepter never leaving Judah was not going to go out and come back void!

I have found that many times people think that the things they do for God doesn't matter much, but to the contrary that is only because they are not looking at the bigger picture of things. Just like many when reading this story only see the miraculous saving of just the three Hebrew boys and not the miraculous saving of the whole Jewish people, because there was only a slight reference mentioned unto it in – Daniel 3: 8. Slight or not, it was still mentioned and carried a greater impact than most knew. Were there some Jews bowing down to the image just to save their lives, they thought? Yes, yes there were, but the question is, would it really have saved their lives in the long run? No, no it would have not. Why, you may ask? Because Satan knew that if any of the Jews were allowed to exist especially of the tribe of Judah, the prophecy and the promise given unto Judah in the form of a blessing, which it was, would come to pass. This is why the enemy wars against the nation of Israel and every Jew in the world today along with warring against the body of Christ which is the church to stop the plans of God from coming to pass. Can he do it? No, but he still tries anyway! Which cause problems for the people of God all over the world, these are the battles we must fight and stand strong in our faith in and obedience unto God in no matter what.

Often when you throw a rock or a pebble into the water, though you may have just thrown in one stone, the effect of that one stone thrown into the water has now caused many ripples to appear in the water. That ripple effect continues moving towards the shore where they stop or to a point where the motion of the ripples start to dissipate in the water. The effect of just that one stone has now caused an even greater effect to begin in something else. Never think the work you do in or for Christ is small. Everything we do in Christ and for Christ carries a greater effect in the spirit!

5

RIGHTEOUS AUTHORITY

"And the princes, governors, and captains, and the king's counselors, being gathered together, saw these men, upon whose bodies the fire had no power, nor was an hair of their head singed, neither were their coats changed, nor the smell of fire had passed on them.

Then Nebuchadnezzar spake, and said, Blessed be the God of Shadrach, Meshach, and Abed-nego, who hath sent His angel, and delivered His servants that trusted in Him, and have changed the king's word, and yielded their bodies, that they might not serve nor worship any god, except their own God." – Daniel 3:27 – 28

Whether these officials of the king's court were summoned there by the king to witness his judgment upon the rebellious young Jewish men for not bowing to the golden image he had set up or just gathered there together of their own free will to witness the event is not stated, but the fact that they were there was providential in itself. All were there to witness the miracle of the supernatural deliverance by God of the three young men from the burning fiery furnace. Many times we see in the word of God, the Lord showing up or intervening on behalf of His people where the question of His authority, power, and the fate of His children are concerned. In Egypt when Pharoah refused to let the people go, asking Moses who is this God that he should let the people go, He challenged God, (Exodus 5: 2 – 12).

The Lord intervened on behalf of Israel in the sending of ten plagues, causing Pharoah to let the people go and finally drowning the pursuing Egyptian army in the Red Sea. God intervened on behalf of Hezekiah when Sennacherib, king over Assyria challenged the Lord God over Israel to save them out of his hands, (2 Chronicles 32: 9 – 21), saying: "Who was there among all the gods of those nations that my fathers utterly destroyed, that could deliver his people out of mine hand, that your God should be able to deliver you out of mine hand?" - 2 Chronicles 32: 14.

Sennacherib, like Nebuchadnezzar, challenged God. How many times have man foolishly in his arrogance challenged God, thinking that the true and living God was just like the powerless man made images and idols that came out of man's imaginations and the fallen angels and demoniac spirits they worshipped. Neither of these kings or Pharaoh understood they were about to encounter the true and living God! Whose authority surpassed anything created being that He is the Creator! Jehoshaphat, when the inhabitants of Moab, Ammon, and Mount Seir rose up against Judah to take them out of their possession, (2 Chronicles 20: 1 – 20), God answered this threat of being destroyed by these three by telling Jehoshaphat through the prophet Jahaziel, that the battle was not theirs' but the Lord's! There are many, many, more circumstances and events in which God answered the challenges of man as to who He is and His ultimate authority, to turn him back unto the truth. Man in his arrogance, vanity, and pride is always trying to challenge God's authority. This is that same mindset that caused Lucifer, or Satan to get kicked out of heaven and sentenced to the lake of fire when the time of judgment comes, him and every angel that followed him! This same mind set the adversary uses to deceive and to influence those who are weak minded, rejecting of God or do not serve the Lord. It reminds me of the passage in Isaiah 14: 12;

> *"How art thou fallen from heaven, O, Lucifer, son of the morning! How art thou cut down to the ground, which didst weaken the nations!" – Isaiah 14: 11*

When you study history you see this very same rebellious influence and challenges against God's authority being carried out by those in leadership positions. Every time Satan has tried to usurp authority over God's people throughout the earth and the centuries, you find he has always been stopped in some way, form or another. Yes he may run for a while, but when God's people came together and prayed standing on, and in their most holy faith in God to deliver and the challenge went out against the Lord God and his authority, God always answered the challenge, and He always showed Himself victorious! What Satan and the arrogant, and the prideful, and the blind, and the power hungry seem to forget, is that when it said in the word of God, in Isaiah 55: 11, the Lord meant every word!

> *"So shall my word be that goeth forth from my mouth: it shall not return unto me void, but shall accomplish that which I please, and it shall prosper in the thing whereto I sent it. "– Isaiah 55: 11*
>
> *"Fear ye not, neither be afraid: have not I told thee from that time, and have declared it? ye are even my witnesses. Is there a God beside me? Yea, there is no God: I know not any." - Isaiah 44: 8*
>
> *"The earth is the LORD'S, and the fullness thereof; the world, and they that dwell therein." – Psalm 24: 1*

No matter how much man lifted up in arrogance, pride and vanity, being influenced by the adversary tries, there is no getting around God. We read later on in Daniel God deals with Nebuchadnezzar because of his arrogance before Him. God gave Nebuchadnezzar a dream concerning a tree that reached unto heaven and spread out to the end of the earth, whereas a watcher, or angel, came down and commanded that the tree be cut down but leave a stump in the earth.

The Watcher further went on to say, let his heart be changed from a man's heart and a beast's heart be given him for seven years and his portion was to be with the beasts in the grass, (Daniel 4: 4 – 16). As we read further in – Daniel 4:28 – 37, we find that this dream given him by God to warn him, did come to pass because Nebuchadnezzar did not take heed to the warning! He continued in his arrogance against God, claiming its greatness by his hands, not recognizing that it was God that allowed him and his kingdom to prosper. Daniel tried to warn him of this in – Daniel 4: 24 - 25;

> *"This is the interpretation, O king, and this is the decree of the most High, which is come upon my lord the king:*
>
> *That they shall drive thee from men, and thy dwelling shall be with the beasts of the field, and they shall make thee to eat grass as oxen, and they shall wet thee with the dew of heaven, and seven times*

shall pass over thee, till thou know that
the most High ruleth in the kingdom of
men, and giveth it to whomsoever he will.

Wherefore, O King, let my counsel be
acceptable unto thee, and break off thy
sins by righteousness, and thine iniquities
by shewing mercy to the poor; if it may be
a lengthening of thy tranquility." – Daniel
4: 24 – 25, 27

Nevertheless, though he was warned, and had seen God manifest Himself in many ways, Nebuchadnezzar in his arrogance still needed convincing. Once again, twelve months later after being given the dream and the warning through the interpretation that Daniel had given him, while walking in the palace, challenged God's righteous authority. Nebuchadnezzar in his arrogance had forgot how that just twelve months before he while speaking to the people, said how great God was and His signs and wonders, how that His kingdom was from generation to generation and that it was an everlasting kingdom! Nebuchadnezzar told the people how that it was God that had performed these signs and wonders toward him, twelve months later, he forgot who made him king and gave him his kingdom.

King Nebuchadnezzar again challenged God when he stood up in his palace and claimed the greatness of the kingdom of Babylon was built by his might and power, not understanding that if God had not of allowed it, it would not have been built at all. This is what Daniel was warning Nebuchadnezzar of when he told him in the interpretation of his dream it is God who rules over the kingdom of men and He gives it to whosoever He will. One of Nebuchadnezzar's main downfalls was his arrogance and pride, in thinking that he had more power and authority than God. When Nebuchadnezzar made the statement verse 28, about God delivering the young men to serve no other god but their God, you can see he still had not yet grasped the truth about the one and only living God, and the fact that there are no other gods like unto Him. He is God and God alone. This way of thinking no doubt led to Nebuchadnezzar, the king, being finally proven that fact after being driven out into the wilderness by his own madness, whereas he ate grass like the beasts of the field, his hair grew as feathers and his nails grew as bird's claws, and for seven years he was made to live this way, away from the presence of man, because of his arrogance and refusal to recognize the one and only true God and His righteous authority in – Daniel 4: 1 – 37, and that there is no other God beside Him and He is due that respect and honor!

6

RECOGNITION

"Therefore I make a decree, That every people, nation, and language, which speak any thing amiss against the God of Shadrach, Meshach, and Abed-nego, shall be cut in pieces, and their houses shall be made a dunghill: because there is no other God that can deliver after this sort.

Nebuchadnezzar the king, unto all people, nations, and languages, that dwell in all the earth; Peace be multiplied unto you.

I thought it good to shew the signs and wonders that the high God hath wrought toward me.

How great are His signs! And how mighty are His wonders! His kingdom is an everlasting kingdom, and His dominion is from generation to generation." – Daniel 3: 29, 4: 1 – 3

How often after some mighty, great, or supernatural act of God, does man come to the realization that they are not dealing with another man, or some idol that is no god, and no power, or some fallen spirit that also is no god, do they give the real and true God some kind of recognition. Here in Nebuchadnezzar's proclamation he still considers God among other gods, just that He is more powerful, (Daniel 4: 2), it is a recognition, but not a full recognition. King Nebuchadnezzar still had not fully submitted himself to the sovereignty of God. Though he recognized the power of God, he still struggled with the sovereignty of God. Still worshipping Babylon's many idols, even though the Lord God had proven before him many times, over and over again that He was and is the only true and sovereign God, and that his gods were no gods and had no power or authority, yet Nebuchadnezzar still struggled within himself accepting this truth.

Today we still have many that struggle with the reality of an all powerful God. We still have men and women worshipping idols and false gods, unfortunately. Witch craft, and the occult practices are still going on, unfortunately man is stilled being fooled by Satan. Man in his arrogance is still challenging God's authority, and power and who He is. Proclaiming or believing he is a god and still wanting to think that they have more power than God almighty and God is still proving Himself as God all powerful and God alone! God's word is still standing no matter how many kings and leaders have come and gone upon this earth, God's word stills stands true! Man goes to his grave and his soul to the destination it has chose while here on this earth, if a person chose rebelliousness against God and rejected salvation through Jesus Christ, eternal death, if they have chosen salvation through Jesus Christ, eternal life.

Nebuchadnezzar after he saw how marvelously the Lord had delivered Shadrach, Meshach, and Abednego, acknowledged that there was no other god that could deliver them the way that the Lord God had delivered them. Then went on to make a decree, much like the decree he had made earlier when he made the decree for all people, nations and tongues at the sound of all the musical instruments to bow down to the golden image that he set up or be thrown into the fiery furnace, now had to back track and decree a new decree. This decree now was telling the same people, nations and tongues that if anyone spoke anything against the God of Shadrach, Meshach, and Abednego would be cut into pieces, and their houses made dunghill. What a difference and a change!

Many times when we think that we are in power and we have the first and last word over how we think things should go, we do not. Often man in his arrogance, and because of some position of authority, or some accomplishment gained, or some financial or business or political position, tends to think that he is more powerful than God. That is the short sightedness of man based in his own sinful flesh. Why is it that man has always got to have a showdown? Why can he not just accept the truth that God is God and not man and there is no other god besides Him. It is like what Jesus said in – Matthew 23: 24;

> *"Ye blind guides which strain at a gnat, and swallow a camel." – Matthew 23: 24*

We will strain at the truth and swallow wholly a lie.

In Genesis it says the woman was deceived, it doesn't say the man was deceived, it said the man was deceived. When Adam was offered the fruit of the knowledge of good and evil, he just ate. Now Adam was given the command by God not to eat of the tree of the knowledge of good and evil and in return he shared the knowledge of that command with the woman. The woman not fully understanding the command was easily deceived, by the serpent who used her non- fully understanding the command against her, but now Adam was a different case, Adam knew. Adam had walked and talked with God in the garden long before Eve was created. He was not deceived, he agreed. When he lost the glory of God which was the light of God that covered him, he found himself naked. What proof of this you say? Genesis 3: 17;

> *"And unto Adam He said, Because thou hast hearkened unto the voice of thy wife, and hast eaten of the tree of which I commanded thee, saying, Thou shalt not eat of it: cursed is the ground for thy sake;*

*in sorrow shalt thou eat of it all the days
of thy life." – Genesis 3: 17*

In the word of God, it says he hearkened, in
other words he listened and did what the woman
said. Adam knew better. In his rebellion against
God's command, he caused the curse to come
on all mankind, which is only broken in Christ.
What was Adam seeking? To be like God, to know
that he did not need to know, not understanding
he was already like God. What was the reason
why he felt like he needed to know evil especially
when he already knew so much holiness and good?
Why would he ever want to know that which has
brought so much sorrow, pain and death. What
would move this man to turn from God and all
His glory, love, and kindness to want to know
the perils and the troubles of evil? Because he
thought it would make him as God. Adam not
understanding, thinking he would be greater than
he already was, thought that eating the fruit would
mean he would be just like God, disobeyed God.
All through the ages there have been men and
women who in wanting to be like God, in their
arrogance and pride have challenged the very God
of heaven and earth just like Satan did and have

had to be corrected, or judged by God as to who is the real God and who has the real and the true righteous authority. God brought Nebuchadnezzar down to be like the beasts of the field eating grass, no mind until seven years passed by, then and only then did God allow him to look up and let his understanding come back unto him. Then he realized that God is God! It left him making this statement and recognition of God in – Daniel 4: 34 – 35, 37;

> *"And at the end of days I Nebuchadnezzar lifted up mine eyes unto heaven, and mine understanding returned unto me, and I blessed the most High, and I praised and honoured Him that liveth for ever, whose dominion is an everlasting dominion, and His kingdom is from generation to generation:*
>
> *And all the inhabitants of the earth are reputed as nothing: and He doeth according to His will in the army of heaven, and among the inhabitants of the earth: and none can stay His hand, or say unto Him, What doest Thou*

Now I Nebuchadnezzar praise and extol and honour the King of heaven, all whose works are truth, and His ways judgment: and those that walk in pride He is able to abase." – Daniel 4: 34 – 35, 37

7

PROMOTION

"Then the king promoted Shadrach, Meshach, and Abed-nego, in the province of Babylon." – Daniel 3: 30

After witnessing the arm of the Lord move so miraculously where the three young men were concerned, also being seen with them in the midst of the fire, and allowing them to come out unsigned and without the smell of smoke unbound. Nebuchadnezzar not only restored them back to their positions in the government from which they had been temporarily deposed due unto the accusation of some of the Chaldeans and also made them governors over the Jewish captives in Babylon.

Even their captive state there is promotion, liberty and vindication given them by God. It begs the question, "If your life is hid in Christ where there is liberty and freedom, as well as promotion, though you may be captive in the eyes of man are you really captive in God?" to that, my answer would be, "No". My answer would be you are merely displaced, and limited in what you can and cannot do for a time being. Now those whose lives are not hid in Christ and are guilty of the captivity, it is captivity.

If you notice in reading the books of Ezra and Nehemiah, the remnant that went back to Israel kept a freedom mentality. The others who stayed behind kept a captive mentality. In the fact that they chose to stay in captivity than to return back home to their own land, strange don't you think? If you were taken out of your land and homes forcibly and not of your own free will and the government of the country in which you were taken captive was willing to let you go, pay your way, give you money to rebuild your city and your homes, provide you protection and supplies for what you needed in order to do just that, plus be willing to give you back everything they had robbed you of, one would think that a person would jump at the opportunity to return home. Yes you may have to deal with a few angry neighbors who may not be glad that you are back because they may have been benefiting off your land while you were predisposed out of it, or they may have assumed some false authority over the few people that had been left behind in the land while the majority was gone because of their being few in number. It could also be a fear of seeing those who returned come to power again, diminishing their power and authority in the land. Whatever the reason, it pales in comparison to being able to come back home and retain ones' life again. It is something worth fighting for ones' place and ones' purpose again. The knowing of who you are and whose you are in respect unto God is worth the effort and the fight if it comes to that. So man would not think that all this is brought about through some assumed greatness on his part, God reminds us in – Psalm 75:6, who is the power and authority behind our being able to be restored back unto a place where we once were in Him.

> *"I said unto the fools, Deal not foolishly:*
> *and to the wicked, Lift not up the horn:*

Lift not up your horn on high: speak not with a stiff neck.

For promotion cometh neither from the east, nor from the west, nor from the south.

But God is the judge: He putteth down one, and setteth up another." – Psalm 75: 4 – 7

God is always sovereign when it comes to the affairs of His children as well as the world. I find that we are always operating in either His divine will or His permissive will. If we are operating in His divine will, God oversees His divinely purposed plans for our lives. He will establish them in us and through us to the glory of His will and He will see it through to its fulfillment. If we are operating in His permissive will, the freedom to choose, that in which we were given when He created man, it is our choice and we have to bear the consequences or results, whether good or bad of the choices we make. Believe it or not, every leader that has ever rose to power whether they knew it or not, always accomplished the purposes of God, whether they were afflicting God's people or promoting them. Babylon was His arm of judgment that was allowed to gain power in order to bring about God's judgment on Israel for their many sins and backsliding ways. Then when that time of judgment was up, God purposed a leader to come into power that would release them and allow them to return to their land. Now, did Cyrus know this? It is said that Daniel may have told him the prophecies that were written about him from Isaiah and Jeremiah, which may have motivated him to release the Jews to return back unto Israel, since Daniel who had been given a high position in the government and was one of the counselors to king Cyrus, might have shared the prophecies concerning the release of the Jewish captives to return back unto their own land and king Cyrus's involvement with this.

> *"In the third year of Cyrus king of Persia a thing was revealed unto Daniel, whose name was called Belteshazzar: and the thing was true, but the time appointed was long: and he understood the thing, and had understanding of the vision."* – *Daniel 10: 1*

Now there is no clear evidence that this is what transpired, it is assumed because of Daniel's position in the kingdom and the fact that king Cyrus kept him on as a counselor to him when he came into power. Now Cyrus was Persian and not a believer so to speak in one God, but, because God's sovereign will or divine will was in play, God saw to it being carried out. Now this falls back on Isaiah 55: 11;

> *"So shall my word be that goeth forth out of my mouth: it shall not return unto me void, but it shall accomplish that which I please, and it shall prosper in the thing whereto I sent it." – Isaiah 55: 11*

The Lord had had already sent the word of prophesy into the earth years before King Cyrus was ever born that he would do just what he did. Thus we can stand on the proven truths of God's word that promotion does not come from the east, the west, or the south, but from God who is the righteous judge of all the earth. That being said, when Nebuchadnezzar was moved to restore the young men back to their prior positions in leadership with nothing lacking, he also gave them positions in the government of the Jewish peoples in Babylon was concerned, so it was a promotion set up by God when the Lord allowed the king to see

Him walking in the midst of the fiery furnace with the young men. No doubt Nebuchadnezzar was so moved as we can tell in the statement he made of no other God could deliver of this sort, seeing how highly God thought of them to appear with them, was moved to give them an even higher position of authority in the kingdom. They may have gone into the fire having lost all, but they came out gaining more than what they lost before they went in. Whenever the Lord steps in on our behalf, we always come out greater than what we were before. God uses challenges like these to promote His people and to put down the enemy of His people, God shows His self all powerful and completely able to deliver His people out of anything and from anything or anyone! God is able! We do not rule by ourselves, not one of us can make ourselves great without God either allowing it or purposing it for His glory! Though it may tarry, wait on it because if God spoke it, it will surely come to pass!

What I like about the book of Job is that in God's discourse in answer to Job's friends and Job, He revealed the universe in its creation as well as the earth and everything therein and its dependency on Him to keep everything in order. If God were to withdraw His power at any time everything would cease to exist. Everything that is exists because of the power of God and the authority of God, all of us ascended into the knowledge of the truth through Jesus Christ being delivered from the stronghold of non- truths or lies, impressed upon us through the adversary and the weakness of our flesh being broken off our thinking and false perceptions of the truth by the acceptance of the real truth through Jesus Christ! Most people on earth only look at God through one light or one view, but as you pray and seek God you find that there are many aspects, views and levels and revelations of the one God that we serve.

There is always more and new revelations and deeper and brighter understanding of things when it comes to understanding the ways, person, power, being, authority, will, etc., of God. If we were able to look through eternity, we would never be able to see all the revelations of God; He is from eternity to eternity! He is Elohim – Father, Son and Holy Ghost, the triune God. All promotion comes from God.

Nebuchadnezzar because he had amassed great authority over the people that he had been allowed to conquer, thought that he was just as powerful as God. When God showed him who really was in power He humbled himself to an extent until God had to take him down personally and he humbled himself for good.

Like Balaam in the book of Numbers, Nebuchadnezzar had learned a powerful lesson that day when he challenged God to save Shadrach, Meshach, and Abednego. He learned you cannot curse whom God has blessed!

"How shall I curse, whom God hath not cursed? Or how shall I defy, whom the LORD hath not defied?" – Numbers 23: 8

When men come against the Most High God and all of His authority with their no authority, they will always loose! Everything we have has been given to us for a time and a season by God.

"To every thing there is a season and a time to every purpose under the heaven:" - Ecclesiastes 3: 1

The Preacher, who is believed to be Solomon, the son of David, king in Jerusalem, (Ecclesiastes 1: 1), was given the gift of wisdom by God when praying for guidance on how to rule Israel, 1 Kings 3: 7 – 11;

"And now, O LORD my God, Thou hast made Thy servant king instead of David my father: and I am but a little child: I know not how to go out or to come in.

And Thy servant is in the midst of Thy people which Thou hast chosen, a great, that cannot be numbered nor counted for multitude.

Give therefore Thy servant an understanding heart to judge Thy people, that I may discern between good and bad: for who is able to judge this Thy so great a people?

And God said unto him, Because thou hast asked this thing, and hast not asked for thyself long life; neither hast asked riches for thyself, nor hast asked the life of thine enemies; but hast asked for thyself understanding to discern judgment;

Behold, I have done according to thy words: lo, I have given thee a wise and understanding heart; so that there was none like thee before thee, neither after thee shall any arise like unto thee." – 1 Kings 3: 7 – 11

Oh that our leaders over the nations would ask such a prayer request from God and mean it from the heart like Solomon son of David did when he found himself faced with running a nation! How great the nations of the world would be under God to this day! But sadly, many go the way of Nebuchadnezzar and try to put themselves in the place of God as far as power and authority goes over the people, to be worshipped like God and end up making the same mistakes the rulers or leaders did when they went beyond their authority over God's people and begun to challenge God and His authority and power. This same mistake Satan made when he was kicked out of heaven and all his followers that believed him instead of the God that made them! He is still impressing this same mind on leaders of countries now, all who would listen to his lies. They all ended up being taken down, brought down or dying off having accomplished nothing but great despair and misery for themselves and those who followed them, if they had not repented and changed their ways.

Daniel in chapter four after interpreting Nebuchadnezzar's dream concerning the great tree that was cut down and its stump left in the earth. It was wet with the dew of heaven and its portion was with the beasts in the grass of the earth, counseled the king Nebuchadnezzar to break off his sins by righteousness and his iniquities by showing mercy to the poor if in hopes it would lengthen his peace or tranquility. One year later, the king walked in his palace and claimed that Babylon was made great by his own power and for the honor of his majesty – Daniel 4: 27 – 30, and while he was yet speaking, God spoke, and king Nebuchadnezzar lost his mind and was driven out of palace into the wilderness whereas he ended up looking like the beasts and eating grass like them for seven years! I say again, all promotion comes from God and not man.

> *"The same hour was the thing fulfilled upon Nebuchadnezzar: and he was driven from men, and did eat grass as oxen, and his body was wet with the dew of heaven, till his hairs were grown like bird's claws.*
>
> *And at the end of the days I Nebuchadnezzar lifted up mine eyes unto heaven, and mine understanding returned unto me, and I praised and honoured Him that liveth for ever, whose dominion is an*

everlasting dominion, and His kingdom
is from generation to generation.

And all the inhabitants of the earth
are reputed as nothing: and He doeth
according to His will in the army of
heaven, and among the inhabitants of
the earth: and none can stay His hand,
or say Him, What doest Thou?" – Danirl
4: 33 – 36

It was only when Nebuchadnezzar looked up at
the end of the seven years and acknowledged God,
did he regain his right mind and was restored unto
his position.

"At the same time my reason returned
unto me; and my counselors and my lords
sought unto me.

Now I Nebuchadnezzar praise and
extol and hour the King of heaven, all
whose works are truth, and His ways
judgment: and those that walk in pride
He is able to abase." – Daniel 4: 36 – 37

Nebuchadnezzar's pride and arrogance caused
him to lose his mind and have to leave his palace,
position, and kingdom to be driven into the

wilderness to eat grass like the beasts of the field. It was when he let go of that pride and arrogance and looked up and acknowledged that God is God and He alone had the power and authority to set up kings and kingdoms and He alone has the power to take them down. Nebuchadnezzar learned and finally understood where true promotion came from. This lesson is still being taught today, but if we make a stand for and in Christ we can come out of any trial, "Without the Smell of Smoke."

REFLECTIONS

Many times in life we are challenged whether or not we are going to stay on the wall of faith and stand for that which is righteous and good before the Lord. Sometimes these challenges come from strangers, sometimes these challenges come from our enemies, sometimes these challenges come from our jobs, our health, our families, our children, our churches, our communities, even our governments, but regardless to where they come from as followers of our Lord and Savior Jesus Christ, we are required to make a stand for God, truth and righteousness, because we know that it is the right thing to do and it is the will of our Father God which is in Heaven, watching daily over His children. It is almost like I can hear in my spirit, the same question the Lord asked in Heaven in – Isaiah 6 chapter;

"Whom shall I send, and who will go for us?" – Isaiah 6: 8

When I think about the reason why the Holy Spirit wanted me to write Without the Smell of Smoke, I can't help but think about my own life, and the many times the Lord has brought me out without the smell of smoke. Many times I have faced challenges in my life that have tested my faith, my belief, and my trust in God to bring me through, out or delivered. Challenges by all rights according to what I was facing or going through, should have taken me down or destroyed me, yet became great testimonies of God's faithfulness, deliverance, grace, power, and authority! Times where my faith in God was challenged as to whether or not God would, or could take power and authority in my lift and over my life to bring me through all of life's challenges that were coming at me.

Whether we know it or not when we make a stand for Christ, whether we are doing it for personal reasons or for national, we are doing it for all! I have found that when we make the righteous choice when we are challenged by Satan as to whether or not God is real in our lives, others by your stand and testimony can take courage and trust God and make a stand for Christ in their lives. We all are given as examples to one another when it comes to making a stand for and in God. Without the smell of smoke came to me after I began to see the strong attack which the adversary had come out against God and the believer's belief in God, the Church and all that the Christian church stood for. All I could hear in the Spirit, was, stand and stand strong, unwavering! It looked and seemed like the church, the body of Christ, was crumbling and our faith and our belief in God was on trial, to see if we would stand up for God. Our faith in God and our rights to serve Him as followers of Christ also being tested. There are times when we are going to be challenged on this, for this is the work of our enemy, Satan to keep the body of Christ weak and confused as to what is true and righteous before God. Just like the enemies of Nehemiah when they saw him building the wall, wanted him to come down so they could stop the work of God because they knew that once the wall and temple were built, worship of God would resume and the power and presence of God would once more reign amongst His people and their enemies would need to beware! Such is the power and the presence of the Spirit of God amongst His people. He is their protection, as well as their provider, their strength, and their sword and shield! He would not forsake them or leave them in the hands of their enemies! He will restore and bring them out without the smell of smoke!

Without the Smell of Smoke, is about God's unfailing faithfulness to His children, His deliverance in times of great trial by the enemy. God's answer when He is challenged, and His unerring ability to bring one out without the smell of smoke or having to ever even look like they have been in a trial of their life! To God be all the Glory!

> *"So shall they fear the name of the LORD from the west, and His glory from the rising of the sun. When the enemy shall come in like a flood, the Spirit of the LORD shall lift up a standard against him.*
>
> *And the redeemer shall come to Zion, and unto them that turn from*

transgression in Jacob, saith the LORD." –
Isaiah 59: 19 - 20

Truly God the Father, Christ our Lord and Saviour, the Holy Spirit and all the host of heaven are our protectors of our faith in God and will stand with us in the fire. They will without a doubt, when we put our faith and trust in them, and stand for truth, for righteousness, and the right to serve our most holy God, our Father and will bring us out without fail, and without the smell of smoke.

ABOUT THE AUTHOR

Dianne Chatman born in Augusta Georgia, 1957 came to know Christ was filled with the Holy Ghost in the year 1980. Called to the ministry in the year 2000, has definitely has had her share of trials, tests and challenges, whereas her Christian faith and belief, and stand of faith has been tested and challenged. Precious sacrifices have been made over and over again in her walk with Christ. Times where she has lost everything, even children. Suffered many health challenges, even challenges to her life whereas her Christian faith and belief were concerned. Through it all, she can testify, that God is able to deliver! And if He chooses not to deliver, He is well worthy of our sacrifice, for the reward is greater than the journey!

Printed in the United States
by Baker & Taylor Publisher Services